APPLE FOR THE TEACHER

THIRTY SONGS FOR SINGING WHILE YOU WORK

The folk artist who made this sculpture was a farmer and logger who had limited education and almost no artistic training. He ran a 300-acre farm, supplemented his income with logging, and suffered serious injuries and illness throughout his life. Yet he managed to produce more than 1,500 objects similar to this sensitive and respectful portrait of a rural schoolteacher.

Schoolmarm, Lavern Kelley, Oneonta, New York, 1988, carved and painted pine, 31 x 7 ½ in. Fenimore Art Museum, Cooperstown, New York.

APPLE FOR THE TEACHER

THIRTY SONGS FOR SINGING WHILE YOU WORK

COLLECTED AND INTRODUCED BY
JANE YOLEN
MUSIC ARRANGED BY ADAM STEMPLE

ART EDITED BY
EILEEN MICHAELIS SMILES

HARRY N. ABRAMS, INC., PUBLISHERS

Designed by Angela Carlino and Vivian Cheng
Production Manager: Jonathan Lopes

Library of Congress Cataloging-in-Publication Data
Yolen, Jane.
Apple for the teacher : thirty songs for singing while you work / Jane Yolen and Adam Stemple.
p. cm.
ISBN 0-8109-4825-7
1. Work songs—Texts. 2. Work songs—History and criticism. 3. Working class—Songs and music.
I. Stemple, Adam. II. Title.

ML54.6.Y67A67 2005
782.42'1593'0268—dc22
2004024404

On the front of the jacket: *Bucks County Farm Scene*, unidentified artist, Doylestown, Pennsylvania, circa 1875, oil on canvas, 24 x 30 in. Collection of the Mercer Museum, Doylestown, Pennsylvania. Photo courtesy of Olde Hope Antiques, Inc., New Hope, Pennsylvania. **On the front flap of the jacket:** *Winter Landscape,* possibly by Joseph Henry Hidley, New York, circa 1860, oil on canvas, 19 x 24 ¼ in. Photo courtesy of Olde Hope Antiques, New Hope, Pennsylvania. **On the spine of the jacket:** *Erie Railroad Quilt,* artist unidentified, Peru, Indiana, 1888, appliquéd cotton, 78 x 73 in. The Museum of Fine Arts, Boston, Massachusetts. **On the back of the jacket:** *Cowboy and Horse Weathervane,* United States, circa 1930, sheet iron, 28 in. Photo courtesy of Harvey Art and Antiques, Evanston, Illinois. **On the back flap of the jacket:** *Cowboy Shooting Gallery Target,* attributed to William F. Mangels Company, Brooklyn, New York, circa 1920, painted cast iron, 60 x 28 x 1 in. Photo courtesy of the Splendid Peasant, Ltd., South Egremont, Massachusetts.

Printed and bound in China
10 9 8 7 6 5 4 3 2 1

Harry N. Abrams, Inc.
100 Fifth Avenue
New York, NY 10011
www.abramsbooks.com

Abrams is a subsidiary of LA MARTINIÈRE
GROUPE

Apples to the following teachers who made a difference in my life: Mrs. Jiler of PS 93; V. Louise Higgins and Senorita Higgins of Staples High School, Westport, Connecticut; Dr. William Van Voris, Dr. Edna Williams, Dr. Joel Dorius, and Dr. Marie Borroff of Smith College; and Dr. Masha Rudman of the University of Massachusetts.

—J.Y.

For Mrs. Rankin, my first and best piano teacher.

—A.S.

This weathervane was made at the A.L. Jewell & Co. ironworks factory in New York in about 1875. To make weathervanes like this, an artist would carve two wooden patterns for each side, then iron molds were made from the wooden patterns. Next, factory workers hammered sheets of copper around the molds to create the two sides of the fireman. Finally, the sides were soldered together to form the whole. This lively figure of a fireman with his horn is the only known example of its kind.

Fireman Weathervane, A.L. Jewell & Co., from Rye firehouse, New York, circa 1875, molded copper, 28 x 14 in. Private collection. Photo courtesy of Olde Hope Antiques, Inc., New Hope, Pennsylvania.

CONTENTS

This picture was painted by an Italian immigrant artist in New Jersey in about 1890. It illustrates a biblical proverb, and shows a cheerful view of a country blacksmith's shop during the late 1800s. The blacksmith smiles at us as he works, while his helper collects swords to be melted down and made into plows for farming.

And They Shall Beat Their Swords into Ploughshares, F. Da Camara, New Jersey, circa 1890, oil on canvas, 17 1/2 x 23 1/2 in. Photo courtesy of David A. Schorsch—Eileen M. Smiles, Woodbury, Connecticut.

This sign was used in the Ford motor car factory in Dearborn, Michigan in the early 1900s. It warned workers, who were anxious to leave the factory at the end of a long day, to be patient and to wait their turn when punching their time clocks.

Walk to Time Clocks, Don't Crowd, factory sign from the Ford Motorcar Company, Dearborn, Michigan, circa 1920, painted wood, 6 ½ x 15 in. Photo courtesy of David A. Schorsch—Eileen M. Smiles, Woodbury, Connecticut.

{INTRODUCTION}

Many members of the insect community, such as ants and bees, are considered hard workers. Elephants in their family groups and wolves in their packs share babysitting duties. Lionesses are the hunters of their clans. Cats help farmers by killing off mice. Dogs can be trained as drug sniffers or as seeing-eyes for blind people. Some monkeys can be taught to help out handicapped humans.

But nowhere in the animal kingdom is the variety of labor greater than among human beings. From the earliest times, when we were merely hunters and gatherers, we were also makers of tools and weapons, keepers of fire, costumers, bonesetters, storytellers, and speakers to the gods.

As human civilization became more and more complex, there were more and more jobs to be done. Now we are not only hunters, but also fisherfolk and farmers and shepherds and dairymen and scientists who breed cattle in test

This group of busy workers was made of metal in about 1900, and would have been mounted on top of a house or barn as a roof ornament. The piece once had a spinning windmill. It is still charming, however, with its glass inlaid windows and mischievous rooster stealing a worm from the fisherman's bait can.

Farm Vignette, unidentified artist, United States, early twentieth century, paint on metal with glass, 27 ½ x 64 x 12 ½ in. Collection of American Folk Art Museum, New York, gift of Dorothea and Leo Rabkin. Photo by John Parnell, New York.

tubes. Now we are not only makers of weapons and tools, but also blacksmiths and ironmongers and steel hammerers and gunsmiths and makers of tanks, stealth bombers, and H-bombs. Not only keepers of fire, but sous chefs and wedding cake bakers and inventors of things like bubblegum, Pepsi, and tofu. Not only costumers, but skinscrapers and needlemakers and bustle designers and high fashion models and the person who invented Nike sneakers. Not only bonesetters, but doctors and neurologists and pediatricians and psychiatrists and registered nurses and orthodontists. Not only storytellers, but writers of best sellers, movie makers, creators of CGI animation, cartoonists, klieg-light specialists, choreographers, news presenters, and pop stars. Not only speakers to the gods, but priests, ministers, rabbis, imams, the pope, and television evangelists.

The list is quite literally endless.

Along the way, humans learned to sing about their work. It made the hard work easier, the scary work friendlier, the dull work livelier, and the long work days shorter.

So Adam Stemple and I—Jane Yolen, at work on my computer—have put together a book about work and songs—thirty songs for thirty different kinds of jobs. Some of the songs are really old and some are brand new. We have included only one song per kind of work, though, or it would be hard labor indeed to carry the book around.

All of these are fun to sing by yourself, or with your fellow workers.

Many workers now are part of labor unions, where the workers band together to bargain for better wages and safer work conditions. There are even labor union songs, though we have not included them here. That would take another book!

The labor movement grew out of the old guild systems, groups of workers in the same trade, such as weaving, who banded together to make rules for the protection of their businesses. American immigrants brought these systems to the United States with them. However, we date the true beginnings of the American labor movement to the 1860s. In 1869, "The Noble and Holy Order of the Knights of Labor" was established in Philadelphia. One of the most important questions the Knights asked was this: "How can the toiler receive a just share of the wealth he creates?"

It is a question that is still being asked today.

Before the days of "The Weather Channel," weathervanes helped people predict the weather through wind patterns. Many weathervanes were mounted with lightning rods to attract lightning in a storm away from nearby houses and trees. Farm animal shapes were the most common weathervanes. Sitting atop a house or barn, a unique and animated weathervane such as this man in the moon would seem to come alive as it moved in the wind.

Man in the Moon Weathervane and Lightening Rod, unidentified artist, Pennsylvania, circa 1880, molded sheet copper and forged iron, 72 x 32 x 10 in. Private Collection. Photo courtesy of Allan Katz Americana, Woodbridge, Connecticut.

Sometimes an everyday object can be transformed into a unique work of art. In the case of this game board, which was made during the late 1800s, the maker painted his or her checkerboard with a fanciful tribute to the stars and planets, and elevated both the object and the player's experience to new heights of imagination.

Checkerboard and Checker Box, unidentified artist; inscribed "Osgood," northeastern United States; late nineteenth century, paint on wood and tin, 21 x 10 in. Collection American Folk Art Museum, New York, promised gift of Patty Gagarin.

ASTRONAUT

{FIRE IN THE SKY}

It would have been impossible, of course, to find an old folk song about an astronaut, since this is such a new job. Jordin Kare, who wrote both the words and music for this song, is a scientist. Prometheus was a demi-god in Greek mythology who made man and gave him fire. Icarus was the Greek boy in myth who, with wings made of birds' feathers and wax, flew too near the sun. The sun's heat melted the wax and Icarus fell to earth. Apollo, Greek god of the sun, was also the name of the American space ship that landed the first man on the moon. Yuri Gagarin was the Russian cosmonaut who was the first man in space. Today women as well as men ride that fire in the sky.

Words & Music by Jordin Kare

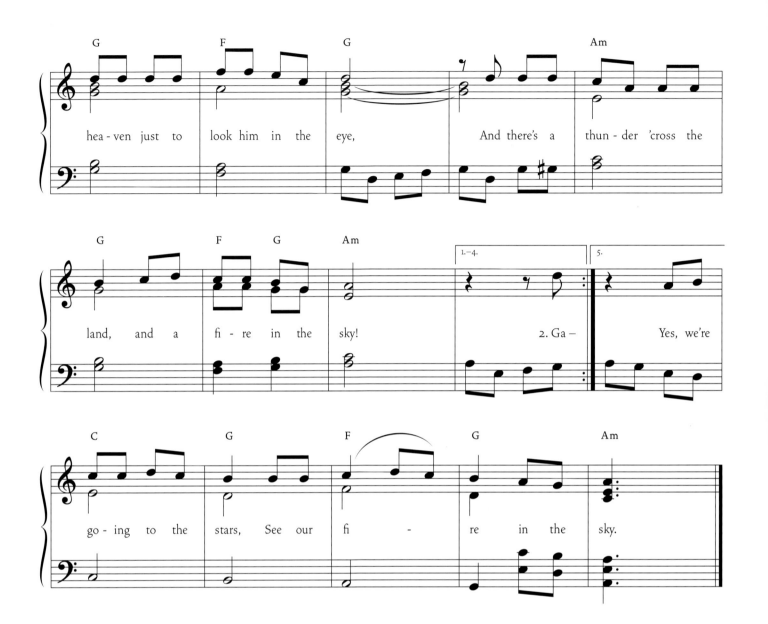

2. Gagarin was the first, back in nineteen sixty-one,
When like Icarus, undaunted, he climbed to reach the sun.
And he knew he might not make it, for it's never hard to die,
But he lifted off the pad and rode a fire in the sky.

3. Yet a higher goal was calling, and we vowed to reach it soon,
And we gave ourselves a decade to put fire on the moon.
And Apollo told the world, "We can do it if we try,"
For there was one small step, and a fire in the sky.

4. Now two decades since Gagarin, twenty years to the day,
We've a shuttle named Columbia to open up the way.
Though they say she's just a truck, she's a truck that's aiming high!
See the big jets burning. See her fire in the sky.

5. Now the rest is up to us. There's a future to be won.
We must turn our faces outward. We will do what must be done.
For no cradle lasts forever. Every bird must learn to fly,
Yes, we're going to the stars. See our fire in the sky.

BARBER

{BARBER, SPARE THOSE HAIRS}

This nineteenth-century music hall song makes fun of college boys trying to grow sideburns, which were then all the rage. Hardly anyone is called a barber these days. Most hair cutters now prefer to be called stylists.

Words by John Love   *Music by Henry Russell*

Yearning and freely (♩ = 96)

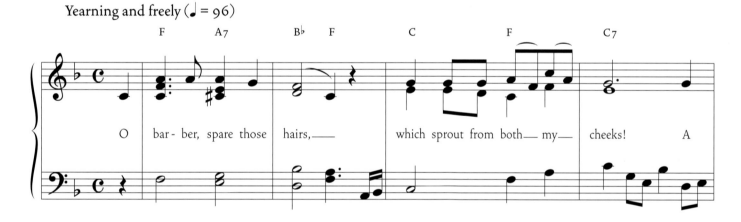

O bar- ber, spare those hairs,___ which sprout from both___ my___ cheeks! A

sol - ace for my cares_____ I have cher - ished them for weeks. They

This elegant portrait was painted in about 1825 in Massachusetts by an artist known as Mr. Wilson. It depicts a debonair young man in his stylish Sunday best. No expense was spared in this man's clothes, where ruffles, patterns, and gems abound. He even sits in a fancy hand-painted chair. He has turned his head just slightly to the side. Do you think he is showing off his fashionable sideburns?

Joseph Brown, Jr. of Gloucester in a Fancy Decorated Chair, attributed to Mr. Wilson, Massachusetts, circa 1825, watercolor, gouache, and ink on paper, 20 3/4 x 18 1/2 in. Collection of Raymond and Susan Egan.

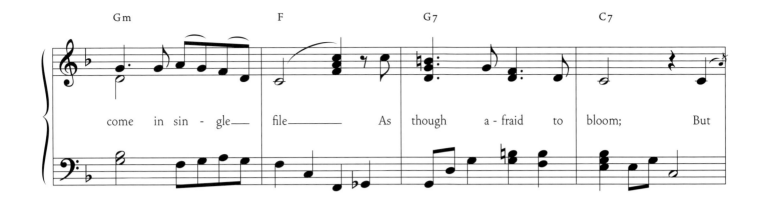

come in sin-gle____ file____ As though a-fraid to bloom; But

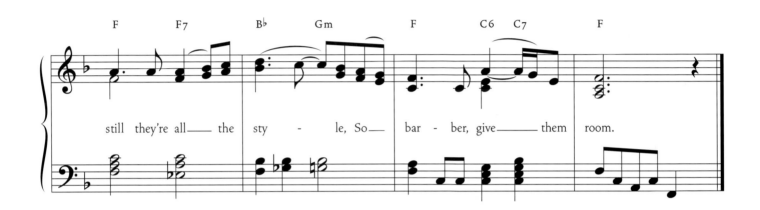

still they're all____ the sty - le, So____ bar-ber, give____ them room.

2. I've reached a Junior's state,
Its dignity and fame,
And though these hairs came late,
They still can honor claim.
With awe the Freshmen see
These proofs of ripening years,
And bow while passing me,
Beset with trembling fears.

3. O, give them yet a year
The strength'ning sap to draw,
For then you need not fear,
They'll grow two inches more.
Then barber, list to me,
And bend unto my cry,
O, let my whiskers be,
Not yet thy calling ply.

4. And when I'm passing near,
T'will be, I'm sure, no wrong,
Your waiting eyes to cheer
With whiskers thick and long.
Now, barber, fare thee well,
The blade put on its shelf,
And ne'er this story tell,
But keep it to yourself.

Lockport on Erie Canal New York. Painted by Mary Keys 1832.

A school girl named Mary Keys painted this picture in 1832. In it, a team of mules is pulling a barge through a lock, a device that lifts or lowers boats to a different level of a canal.

Lockport on the Erie Canal, Mary Keys, America, 1832, watercolor on paper, 15 ¼ x 20 ¼ in. Munson-Williams—Proctor Arts Institute Museum of Art, Utica, New York.

BARGEE

{THE ERIE CANAL}

The Erie Canal, completed in 1825, was a man-made waterway that connected all the Great Lakes with the Atlantic, allowing river barges to carry both passengers and freight to places like Illinois, Wisconsin, and Michigan and back. The barges were pulled by horses or mules, who walked on a towpath beside the canal. The mules, and thus the barges, moved at a speed of about four miles per hour. The boat drivers were known as bargees, and sometimes things were so quiet along the route, they made up songs like this one. The mule driver—or "hoggie"—would be the first to know when a low bridge was ahead. He would shout out, "Low bridge, everybody down," and passengers and cabin crew all had to lie flat on their stomachs until the boat passed under the bridge. Not everyone listened, to their great distress.

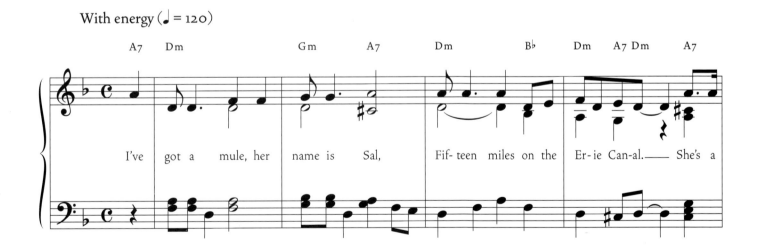

With energy (♩ = 120)

I've got a mule, her name is Sal, Fif-teen miles on the Er-ie Can-al.—— She's a

2. We better get along on our way, ol' gal,
Fifteen miles on the Erie Canal.
'Cause you bet your life I'd never part with Sal,
Fifteen miles on the Erie Canal.
Git up there, mule, here comes a lock,
We'll make Rome 'bout six o'clock,
One more trip an' back we'll go,
Right back home to Buffalo.
(Chorus)

This picture depicts two young boys who work as chimney sweeps. The artist has captured the poverty and loneliness of these hard-working children by depicting them on the city streets in which they often lived.

Chimney Sweeps, William P. Chappel, New York, 1870s, The Metropolitan Museum of Art, New York. The Edward W.C. Arnold Collection of New York Prints, Maps, and Pictures bequest of Edward W.C. Arnold, 1954.

CHIMNEY SWEEP

{CHIMNEY SWEEPER}

This American street cry would have been sung as an advertisement by a chimney sweep offering his services to anyone who needed their chimneys cleaned of soot. Chimney sweeps were often boys small enough to fit in a foot-wide shaft. They also cleaned ovens back in the days when ovens were not electric, but were heated with firewood and coals.

2. Chimney Sweeper, clean out yo' oven,
Chimney Sweeper know why yo' oven won't draw.

3. Chimney Sweeper, he sho' can make
Yo' oven bake, bake, bake a mighty fine cake.

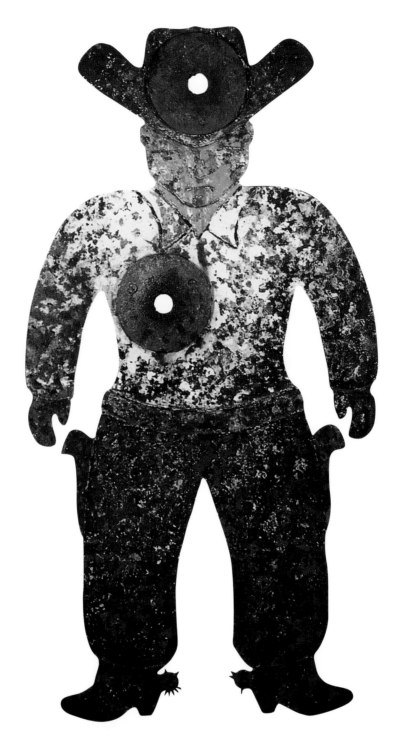

This cowboy was used as a shooting gallery target in Brooklyn, New York, during the 1920s and 1930s. A little tough guy, this painted iron figure evokes the stereotypical cowboy of the Wild West novels that were so popular with children during the early 1900s.

Cowboy Shooting Gallery Target, attributed to William F. Mangels Company, Brooklyn, New York, circa 1920, painted cast iron, 60 x 28 x 1 in. Photo courtesy of the Splendid Peasant, Ltd., South Egremont, Massachusetts.

COWBOY

{GIT ALONG, LITTLE DOGIES}

One of the most popular cowboy trail songs, this celebrates that most typical activity of cowboy life: rounding up and branding cattle, and driving them to market. A "dogie" is a stray, motherless calf. A "chuck wagon" is a wagon equipped for cooking and serving meals along the trail. Another term for cowboy is "cow puncher."

2. It's early in spring that we round up the dogies.
We mark 'em and brand 'em and bob off their tails.
We round up our horses and load the chuck wagon,
And then throw the dogies out onto the trail.
(Chorus)

3. It's whoopin' and yellin' and a-drivin' them dogies,
Oh, how I wish that you would go on.
It's a-whoopin' and punchin' and go-on, little dogies,
For you know Wyoming will be your new home.
(Chorus)

4. Some cowboys go up to the trail just for pleasure,
But that's where they get it most awfully wrong,
For nobody knows all the trouble they give us
As we drive those little old dogies along.
(Chorus)

This sheet-metal cowboy weathervane was made in about 1930. It is an example of how revealing a simple silhouetted image can be. The maker of this weathervane captured the galloping motion of the horse as well as the eagerness of the cowboy with the use of simple lines.

Cowboy and Horse Weathervane, United States, circa 1930, sheet iron, 28 in. Photo courtesy of Harvey Art and Antiques, Evanston, Illinois.

This textile picture was sewn by a woman named Ethel Wright Mohamed, who worked in a whimsical style. She created a series of brightly stitched pictures chronicling folk and family life in her rural southern town. In this scene, the mother is being assisted by an African American woman, who was probably a midwife. Up until the early twentieth century, it was common for babies born in rural areas to be delivered by midwives, women knowledgeable about childbirth, rather than doctors. African American midwives enjoyed a long tradition as highly-skilled medical and spiritual advisors in their communities.

The New Baby, Ethel Wright Mohamed, Mississippi, circa 1965, cotton yarns embroidered on linen, 28 x 21 ½ in. Copyright © Ethel Wright Mohamed. Photo courtesy of the Ethel Wright Mohamed Stitchery Museum, Belzoni, Mississippi.

DOCTOR

{ THE DOCTOR SONG }

This brand-new song starts with a nursery rhyme. You can tell the song is new because no one in nursery-rhyme days would have known what a virus was. Nor would they have had a woman doctor.

Words by Jane Yolen

Music by Adam Stemple

♩ = 90

Doc - tor, doc - tor, please come quick, My lit - tle boy is sick, sick, sick.

Doc - tor comes, puts her bag on the dress - er, Out come the pills and the tongue de - press - or.

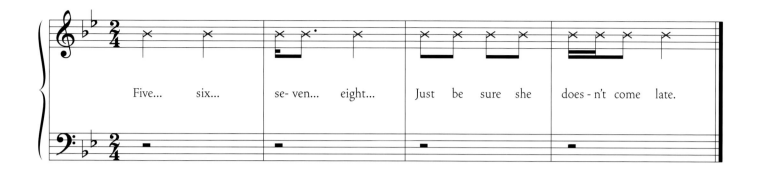

Five... six... se-ven... eight... Just be sure she does-n't come late.

SILAS CUMMINGS.
PRACTICE. AUGUST 1830.

2. The doctor goes, but the virus stays
For days and days and days and DAYS.
Next I get sick, and my man does too,
And the dog and the cat before we're through.
The doctor returns with a bottle of pills,
A new prescription, and a great big bill.
(Chorus)

In this watercolor, we catch a glimpse into the office of a nineteenth-century American doctor. Here he is attending to a patient who is suffering with a wounded arm. The artist was the doctor himself, and this watercolor decorated the front of the medical school notes he kept while he studied at Dartmouth College in New Hampshire.

Doctor Operating, Silas Cummings, Fitzwilliam or Hanover, New Hampshire, probably 1824–1830. Watercolor, pencil, and ink on woven paper, 9 5/8 x 7 13/16 in. Abby Aldrich Rockefeller Folk Art Museum, Colonial Williamsburg Foundation, Williamsburg, Virginia.

This painting is by Bill Traylor, a southern folk artist who lived from 1852 to 1949. He was born a slave and worked on a farm in Alabama before and during the Civil War. After the Civil War, he continued to work on the farm as a free man and a sharecropper. From 1939 to 1942, while living in Montgomery, Alabama, Traylor suddenly began to paint, and is said to have made as many as 1,500 works of art during that time.

Man with a Plow, Bill Traylor, Montgomery, Alabama, circa 1939–1942, poster paint and pencil on paperboard, 15 x 25 3/4 in. Collection of American Folk Art Museum, New York, promised gift of Ralph Esmerian.

FARMER

{THE FARMER IS THE MAN}

This song arose in midwestern America in the 1880s, when farmers were meeting in grange halls to complain about low prices, hard work, and how the middle man was getting all the money from the produce. Even with bigger machines and larger farms, with trucks instead of wagons, nothing much has changed for the farmer a hundred plus years later!

Plaintive yet bouncy (♩ = 110)

When the farm - er comes to town With his wa - gon bro - ken down, Oh, the

far - mer is the man who feeds them all.___ If you'll on - ly look and see, I___

2. When the lawyer stands around,
While the butcher cuts a pound,
Oh, the farmer is the man who feeds them all.
And the preacher and the cook
Go a-strolling by the brook,
Oh, the farmer is the man who feeds them all.

The farmer is the man,
The farmer is the man,
Lives on credit till the fall.
With the interest rates so high,
It's a wonder he don't die,
For the mortgage man's the one who gets it all.

This colorful and detailed painting gives us an idyllic look at a late-nineteenth-century Pennsylvania farmstead. The beautifully appointed house and garden tell us that this is a prosperous farm. The scene is bustling with activity—harvesting, planting, and caring for livestock. We can even see the shrewd and successful farmer in the foreground talking to another man—possibly a middleman who will sell the farmer's goods at market.

Bucks County Farm Scene, Doylestown, Pennsylvania, circa 1875, oil on canvas, 24 x 30 in. Collection of the Mercer Museum, Doylestown, Pennsylvania. Photo courtesy of Olde Hope Antiques, Inc., New Hope, Pennsylvania.

This colorful and detailed portrayal of a rural farmstead was painted by a woman named Mattie Lou O'Kelley in 1976. Her naïve and nostalgic paintings often depict idealized views of southern life and work. In this example, the bright colors, circles, dots, and simple shapes the artist used contribute to the happy mood of the scene. The people in the painting are so cheerful that we can almost hear them singing and whistling while they work.

Off to Fish in the Cotton Picking Season, Mattie Lou O'Kelley, Georgia, 1976, acrylic on canvas, 24 x 30 in. From *Mattie Lou O'Kelley, Folklorist*, by Mattie Lou O'Kelley. Copyright © 1989 by Mattie Lou O'Kelley. By permission of Little, Brown and Company.

FIELD HAND

{Cotton Needs Pickin'}

This song has been adapted from a Florida song, though variations have been found all over the southern United States. Field hands were not always black slaves, but whites as well, and both labored side by side under the burning sun. It was a thankless job, made worse by the conditions under which they worked. Still, when machines began to do the job, many field hands were thrown out of what was—in many cases—the only work they knew. Note that "goosin'" means to pick carelessly. Up until the 1960s, African-American men were called "Uncle" and women "Aunt," but these were condescending names.

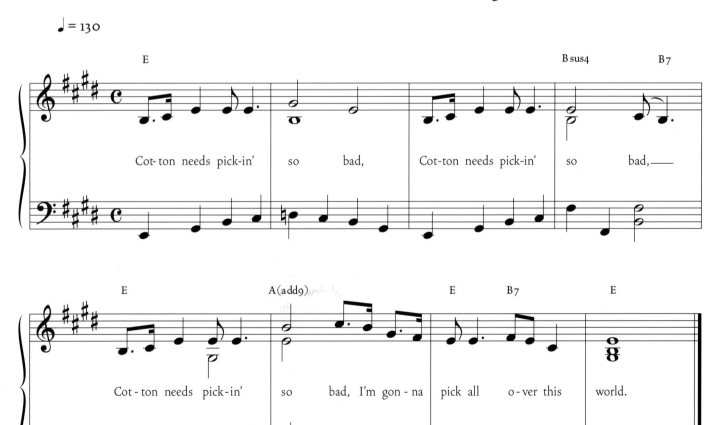

(More verses on next page.)

2. When boss sold that cotton
I asked him for my half,
He told me I done chopped out
My half with the grass.

3. Boss said, "Uncle Billy,
I think you done real well
To pay your debts with cotton
And have your seeds to sell."

4. I sold them seeds this mornin'
For five whole cents a peck
And brought myself a handkerchief
To wind around my neck.

5. Boy, stop goosin' that cotton,
You best take some care.
Make haste, you lazy rascal,
And bring that row from here.

HAULING THE WHOL

This watercolor was made by a silhouette artist, or cut-paper portrait artist, named William Henry Brown, who worked in Mississippi during the 1830s and 1840s. It depicts cotton plantation field hands carrying a week's harvest to market. The artist has captured the barefooted strength and dignity of this family of workers as they carry out this arduous task together.

Hauling the Whole Weeks Picking, William Henry Brown, circa 1842, watercolor on paper collaged on heavy paper; two parts, 19 1/4 x 28 1/8 in. and 19 3/8 x 24 7/8 in. The Historic New Orleans Collection, New Orleans, Louisiana.

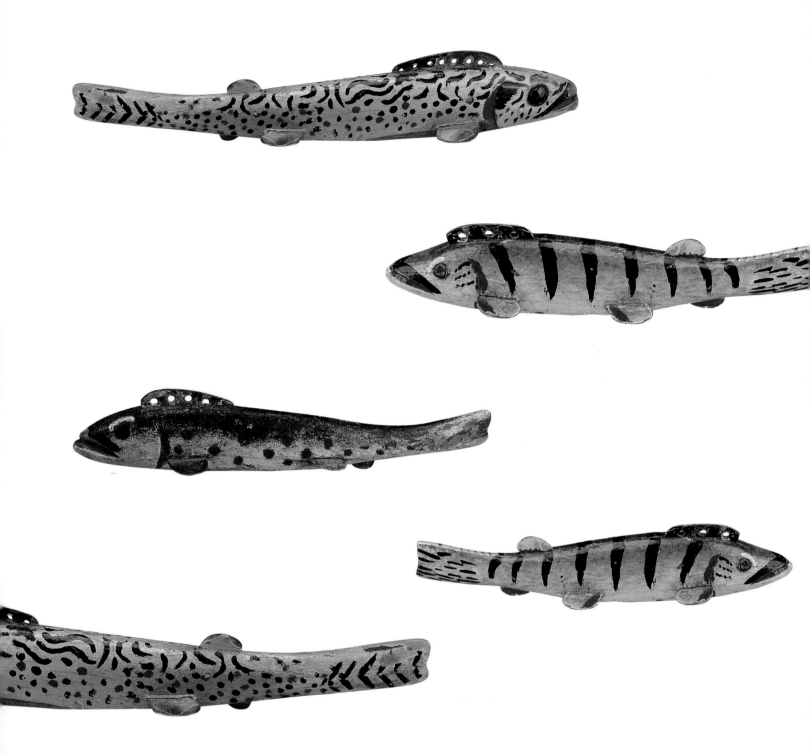

These charming little fish have a whimsical quality due to their small size and brightly colored painted decoration. They are, however, realistic likenesses of their species, made as ice-fishing lures or decoys. They were made in Michigan during the 1930s by a prolific craftsman and fisherman named Oscar Peterson, and they are highly prized by collectors today.

Perch, Brook Trout, and Brown Trout Decoys, Oscar "Pelee" Peterson (1887–1951), Cadillac, Wexford County, Michigan, 1935–1944, paint on wood and metal, 1 x 5 ¹/₈ x 1 ³/₁₆ in. Collection of American Folk Art Museum, New York, gift of Lori Zabar in memory of Selma Segal. Photo by John Parnell, New York.

FISHERMAN

{BOSTON COME-ALL-YE}

This is a forecastle song that arose within the New England fishing fleets in the eighteenth century. There are many interesting words in this song—loft, sheets, tack, topsail, main-chains, poop—that have to do with sailing and fishing.

With a great lilt (♩ = 170)

Come all ye young sail-or-men lis-ten to me,—— I'll sing you a song of the fish of the sea. Then blow ye winds west-er-ly, wes-ter-ly blow,—— we're bound to the south-ward, so stead-y she goes.

★ 41 ★

(More verses on next page.)

2. Oh, first come the whale, the biggest of all,
He clumb up aloft and let every sail fall.
(Chorus)

3. And next come the mack'rel with his striped back;
He hauled aft the sheets and boarded each tack.
(Chorus)

4. Then come the porpoise with his short snout,
He went to the wheel, calling, "Ready! About!"
(Chorus)

5. Then comes the smelt, the smallest of all,
He jumped to the poop and sung out, "Topsail, haul!"
(Chorus)

6. The herring came saying, "I'm king of the seas,
If you want any wind, I'll blow you a breeze."
(Chorus)

7. Last came the flounder, as flat as the ground,
Says: "Dang yer eyes, herring, now mind how ye sound."
(Chorus)

This hooked rug reveals the sense of humor of its maker. It portrays a life-and-death struggle of man and nature, and yet the scene is both charming and silly, with figures tumbling through the sky as they are being thrown from their ship. The rug was made in Nantucket, Massachusetts, the nineteenth-century whaling capital of the world.

Nantucket Whaling Scene Hooked Rug, Nantucket, Massachusetts, circa 1890–1900, fabric hooked on burlap, 18 ¹/₂ x 63 in. Photo courtesy of Austin T. Miller Antiques, Columbus, Ohio.

This picture was made by Denise Allen, a contemporary folk artist working in New York. Using textiles, markers, crayons, paints, pencils, pens, buttons, scraps of clothing, and other interesting objects, Allen makes textiles and collages. Like the folk artists of early America, Allen has not had formal artistic training; instead she says her collages "create themselves."

Beans and Cornbread, Denise Allen, New York, 1998, mixed-media textile collage. © Denise Allen, licensed by VAGA, New York, New York.

HOUSEWIFE

{OLD GRUMBLE}

This American version of an old folk song dates back to 1825. It has been called variously "John Grumble," "Old Grumbler," and "Equinoctial and Phoebe," and is based on an even older folk song that in England goes back to the time of King Henry VII. It is also related to a type of tale that has been especially popular in English-speaking countries, one in which family members trade places in the household with disastrous results, known by folktale scholars as tale type 1408. This song shows that even though we have many different devices to help with housework these days, it is still a more difficult job to do right than most folks think.

Rollicking ($\quarternote$ = 100)

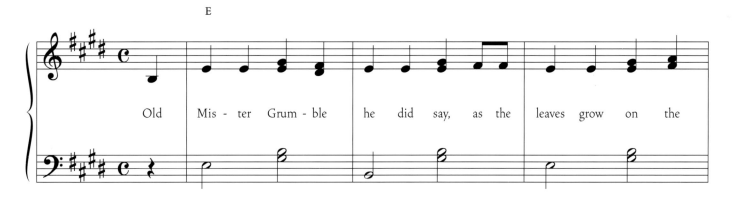

Old Mis - ter Grum - ble he did say, as the leaves grow on the

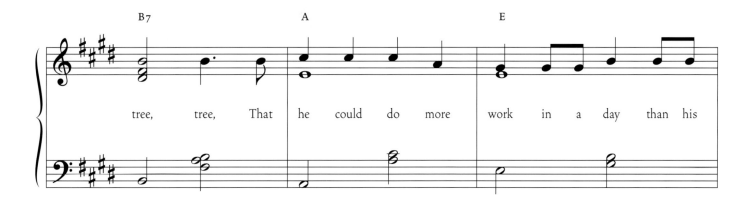

tree, tree, That he could do more work in a day than his

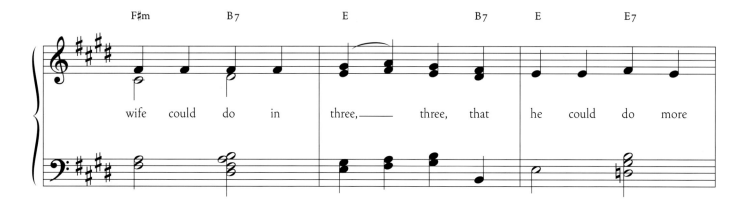

wife could do in three,——— three, that he could do more

work in a day than his wife could do in three.

2. Mistress Grumble she did say,
"You may do it now, now.
You may do the work of the house,
I'll go follow the plow, plow,
You may do the work of the house,
I'll go follow the plow.

3. "You must milk the brindled cow,
For fear that she'll go dry, dry,
You must feed the little pig
That stands within the sty, sty,
You must feed the little pig
That stands within the sty.

4. "You must churn the crock of cream,
That stands within the frame, frame,
And you must watch the fat in the pot
Or it'll go up in a flame, flame,
And you must watch the fat in the pot
Or it'll go up in flame.

5. "You must reel the skein of yarn
That I spun yesterday, day,
You must watch the speckled hen
Or she will run away, way,
You must watch the speckled hen
Or she will run away.

6. Mistress Grumble took the whip,
Went to follow the plow, plow.
Master Grumble took the pail
And went to milk the cow, cow,
Master Grumble took the pail
And went to milk the cow.

7. The cow she kicked, the cow she jumped,
The cow she curled up her nose, nose,
She hit Old Grumble a lick on the chin
And the blood ran down to his toes, toes,
She hit Old Grumble a lick on the chin
And the blood ran down to his toes.

This amusing and highly animated trade sign hung outside a butcher's shop during the first half of the nineteenth century. It is the great-grandfather of the advertisements we see today on TV, and it was just as effective at selling its product. A trade sign like this one, with its eye-catching graphic appeal and high-quality workmanship was able to announce to the public what the shop was selling, as well as attract customers and advertise the success of the enterprise—all in a single image.

Trade Sign for a Butcher's Shop, unidentified artist, American, circa 1835, carved and painted wood.

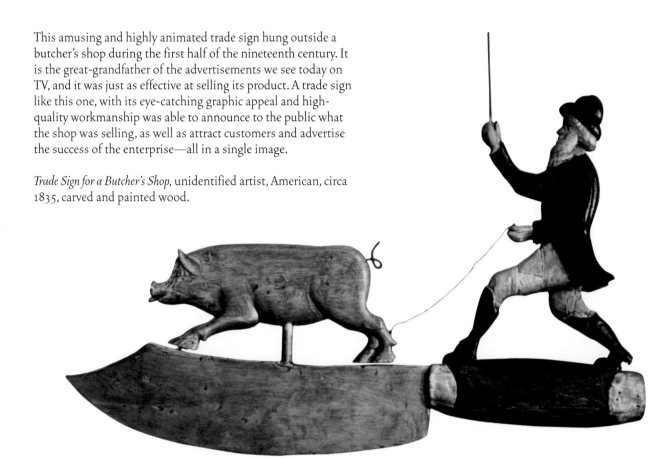

8. He went to feed the little pig
That stood within the sty, sty.
He hit his head against the beam
And his brains began to fly, fly,
He hit his head against the beam
And his brains began to fly.

9. He went to churn the crock of cream
That stood within the frame, frame,
But he forgot the fat in the pot
And it all went up in flame, flame,
But he forgot the fat in the pot
And it all went up in flame.

10. He went to reel the skein of yarn
That his wife spun yesterday, day,
But he forgot the speckled hen
And she did run away, way,
But he forgot the speckled hen
And she did run away.

11. He looked to the east, he looked to the west,
He looked up to the sun, sun,
He swore it was a very long day,
And his wife would never come home, home,
He swore it was a very long day,
And his wife would never come home.

12. Old Mistress Grumble she came home
And found him looking sad, sad.
She clicked her heels and clapped her hands
And said that she was glad, glad,
She clicked her heels and clapped her hands
And said that she was glad.

13. Old Master Grumble he could see
As the leaves grew on the tree, tree,
That his wife could do more work in a day
Than he could do in three, three,
That his wife could do more work in a day
Than he could do in three.

HUNTER

{Let's Go A-Huntin'}

This silly song began its life in England. The hunters in the original song were after a small bird called a wren. Once the song got to America, the hunters were after different game. While at one time most of the meat people ate came from hunting, today such game hunting is rare, and most table meat comes from farms.

With a jaunty swing (♩ = 155)

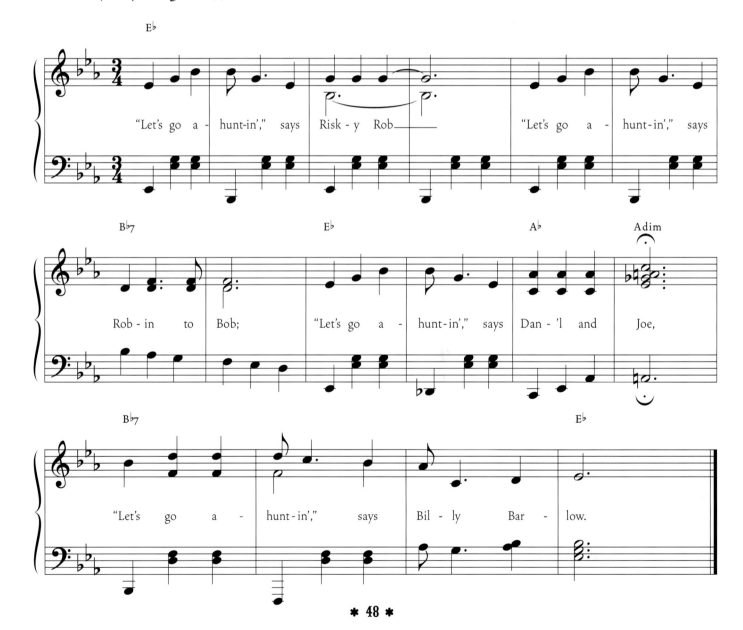

"Let's go a - hunt-in'," says Risk-y Rob___ "Let's go a - hunt-in'," says Rob - in to Bob; "Let's go a - hunt-in'," says Dan - 'l and Joe, "Let's go a - hunt-in'," says Bil - ly Bar - low.

2. "What shall I hunt?" says Risky Rob;
"What shall I hunt?" says Robin to Bob;
"What shall we hunt for?" says Dan'l and Joe;
"Hunt for a rat," says Billy Barlow.

3. "How shall we take him?" says Risky Rob;
"How shall we take him?" says Robin to Bob;
"How shall we take him?" says Dan'l and Joe;
"Borry a gun," says Billy Barlow.

4. "How shall we haul him?" says Risky Rob;
"How shall we haul him?" says Robin to Bob;
"How shall we haul him?" says Dan'l and Joe;
"Borry a cart," says Billy Barlow.

5. "How shall we divide him?" says Risky Rob;
"How shall we divide him?" says Robin to Bob;
"How shall we divide him?" says Dan'l and Joe;
"How shall we divide him?" says Billy Barlow.

6. "I'll take the shoulder," says Risky Rob;
"I'll take the side," says Robin to Bob;
"I'll take the ham," says Dan'l and Joe;
"Tail bone mine," says Billy Barlow.

7. "How shall we cook him?" says Risky Rob;
"How shall we cook him?" says Robin to Bob;
"How shall we cook him?" says Dan'l and Joe;
"How shall we cook him?" says Billy Barlow.

8. "I'll broil the shoulder," says Risky Rob;
"I'll fry the side," says Robin to Bob;
"I'll boil the ham," says Dan'l and Joe;
"Tail bone raw," says Billy Barlow.

In this sculpture, which was carved and painted in about 1875, we are reminded of the rugged life on the American frontier. The earliest Americans had no other way to feed their families than to go out into the wild and hunt for their supper. In this case, the hunter has been successful and has caught a jackrabbit, possibly for Sunday dinner. His dog looks especially happy, anticipating his share of the meal.

Hunter with Dog and Game, unidentified artist, American, circa 1875–1900, carved and painted wood, height six in. From The Henry Ford, Dearborn, Michigan.

This painting was done in New Jersey during the late seventeenth century. It depicts its seemingly regal subjects on horseback during a hunting party. The people in the painting look like English nobles, and this was no accident. It is just as the subjects saw themselves—as transplanted English aristocracy, the landed gentry of the New World. Unlike the silly men in the song, these serious fellows are certainly hunting foxes.

The Hunting Party, unidentified artist, Communipaw (Jersey City), New Jersey, late seventeenth to early eighteenth century, oil on canvas, 25 3/4 x 27 1/8 in. The Metropolitan Museum of Art, New York, gift of Mr. and Mrs. Samuel Schwartz, 1979.

During the late 1800s and early 1900s, race horses and jockeys enjoyed renown similar to the star athletes of today. The speed and grace of thoroughbred race horses were well appreciated, as were the skills of professional jockeys. Try to imagine this jockey weathervane on top of a stable on a windy day—racing through the wind!

Horse and Jockey Weathervane, attributed to J.W. Fiske Ironworks, New York, circa 1880, molded copper and cast zinc, gilt and painted, length 36 in. Private collection. Photo courtesy of David A. Schorsch—Eileen M. Smiles American Antiques, Woodbury, Connecticut.

JOCKEY

{Stewball}

There are many variants of this song, which began in England. It has traveled throughout the English-speaking world to find a particularly happy home in southern America, as a kind of country-western song. Though the singer of this particular song is a man, there are women jockeys as well.

With grandiose certainty (♩ = 104)

Stew - ball was a good____ horse____ He wore a high

head,____ And the mane on his fire - top

Was as fine as silk thread.____

(More verses on next page.)

2. Come all you brave gamblers,
Wherever you are,
Don't bet all your money
On that pretty gray mare.

3. Most likely she'll stumble,
Most likely she'll fall,
But you'll never lose money
On my noble Stewball.

4. As they were a-riding
'Bout halfway around,
That grand mare did stumble
And fell on the ground.

5. And away out yonder,
Ahead of them all
Came a-prancing and dancing
My noble Stewball.

6. I rode him in England,
I rode him in Spain,
And I never did lose, boys.
I always did gain.

Quilt-making has always been a popular American craft. Early American quilts were made by women and schoolgirls, who stitched pieces of different fabrics together to create unique designs. Quilts made with pieces of fabric of random shapes, patterns, and colors are called "Crazy" quilts. The maker of this quilt used the Crazy pattern as a background for her elegant equestrian picture.

Equestrian Crazy Quilt, unidentified artist, possibly New York, 1880–1900, silk, velvet, and cotton with cotton embroidery, 92 x 61 ½ in. Collection American Folk Art Museum, New York, gift of Mr. and Mrs. James D. Clokey III.

LAUNDRY WORKER

{Dashing Away with the Smoothing Iron}

This song originally came from England, where it was sometimes called "Driving Away with the Smoothing Iron." Laundry work was done within households. In poorer families, it was the mother and daughters who did the work. In the richer houses, maids were the ones who spent hours (and days) doing the washing, rinsing, and ironing. Machines for this kind of work were not invented until the nineteenth century, and did not become widely available until the early twentieth century.

This elaborate quilt was made by Lucinda Ward Honstain in Brooklyn, New York, in 1867, just after the Civil War. The quilt is made up of a series of squares like this one, depicting different scenes of domestic, work, and political life at that time. As a whole, the quilt reflects its maker's hope for the bright future of her war-torn country, and her faith in its leaders and people. This scene of a woman hard at work cleaning laundry reflects the artist's view of hard-working people, particularly women, as the strength and backbone of America.

Civil War Reconciliation Quilt, Lucinda Ward Honstain, Brooklyn, New York, 1867, appliquéd and embroidered cotton, 100 x 88 in. Collection of International Quilt Study Center, University of Nebraska–Lincoln.

she was neat and will - ing, oh, a - pick - ing up her lin - en clothes.

Dash - ing a - way with the smooth - ing iron, Dash - ing a - way with the

smooth - ing iron, she stole my heart a - way.

2. 'Twas on a Tuesday morning
When I beheld my darling,
Oh, she was fair and charming
In ev'ry high degree.
Yes, she was neat and willing, oh,
A-soaping of her linen clothes.
(Chorus)

3. 'Twas on a Wednesday morning
When I beheld my darling,
Oh, she was fair and charming
In ev'ry high degree.
Yes, she was neat and willing, oh,
A-starching of her linen clothes.
(Chorus)

(*More verses on next page.*)

4. 'Twas on a Thursday morning
When I beheld my darling,
Oh, she was fair and charming
In ev'ry high degree.
Yes, she was neat and willing, oh,
A-hanging out her linen clothes.
(Chorus)

5. 'Twas on a Friday morning
When I beheld my darling,
Oh, she was fair and charming
In ev'ry high degree.
Yes, she was neat and willing, oh,
A-rolling down her linen clothes.
(Chorus)

6. 'Twas on a Saturday morning
When I beheld my darling,
Oh, she was fair and charming
In ev'ry high degree.
Yes, she was neat and willing, oh,
Ironing of her linen clothes.
(Chorus)

7. 'Twas on a Sunday morning
When I beheld my darling,
Oh, she was fair and charming
In ev'ry high degree.
Yes, she was neat and willing, oh,
A-wearing of her linen clothes.
(Chorus)

This sign was used to advertise the services of a steam laundry shop in upstate New York in about 1900. This no-frills trade sign is representative of the great age of American immigration—hard-working times when shops and factories employed the waves of immigrant workers who came to this country from China and Europe.

Steam Laundry Trade Sign, V. P. Godfrey, New York, circa 1890, painted wood panel, 16 ½ x 31 in. Photo courtesy of Austin T. Miller Antiques, Columbus, Ohio.

LOGGER

{THE FROZEN LOGGER}

This tall-tale song has become a summer camp favorite. It was also popularized by the band the Grateful Dead in the 1970s. A logger cuts down trees for lumbering. A mackinaw is a heavy woolen coat, often made out of blanket cloth.

Words & Music by James Stephens

Playfully (♩. = 90)

As I sat down one eve-ning_____ with - in a small ca - fé,_____ a for - ty year old wait-ress_____ to me these words did say:_____

 (More verses on next page.)

2. "I see you are a logger
And not a common bum,
For no one but a logger
Stirs his coffee with his thumb.

3. "My lover was a logger,
There's none like him today;
If you poured whisky on it,
He'd eat a bale of hay.

4. "He never shaved the whiskers
From off his horny hide,
But he drove them in with a hammer
And bit 'em off inside.

5. "My logger came to see me
'Twas on one freezing day.
He held me in a fond embrace
That broke three vertebrae.

6. "He kissed me when we parted,
So hard he broke my jaw.
I could not speak to tell him
He'd forgot his mackinaw.

7. "The last I saw my logger
He was sauntering through the snow,
A-going gaily homeward
At forty-eight below.

Children growing up in rural America during the 1800s played mostly with handmade dolls and toys like this logger doll. Someone, possibly the child's father, carved the head, face, and hands from some pieces of maple wood. Then someone, possibly the child herself, made the doll's clothes from homespun linens. Throughout its life, this doll has been lovingly cared for and preserved by its young owners.

Woodsman Doll, artist unknown, New York, circa 1860, carved and painted wood, homespun linen, and cotton clothing, 12 in. high. Photo courtesy of David A. Schorsch—Eileen M. Smiles American Antiques, Woodbury, Connecticut.

8. "The weather tried to freeze him,
It tried its level best,
At one hundred degrees below zero
He buttoned up his vest.

9. "It froze clear down to China,
It froze to the stars above,
At one thousand degrees below zero
It froze my logger love.

10. "They tried in vain to thaw him,
And if you believe me, sir,
They made him into axe-blades
To chop the Douglas fir.

11. "And so I lost my true love
And to this café I did come,
And here I wait till someone
Stirs his coffee with his thumb."

The cold, hard life of nineteenth-century workers in the logging industry is captured in this painting of a New York state forest, painted in about 1860. The cold and lonely life is conveyed through the grayness of the light, and the single sled which travels alone through the desolate forest.

Winter Landscape, possibly by Joseph Henry Hidley, New York, circa 1860, oil on canvas, 19 x 24 ¼ in. Photo courtesy of Olde Hope Antiques, New Hope, Pennsylvania.

In this painting, the artist has given us a bird's eye view of the scene, as if we were up in the clouds looking down at the tiny people working in the town below. We almost need a magnifying glass to see the intricate details of daily life, and yet we also get a sense of the larger scale of the entire rural landscape from our elevated viewpoint. During the 1800s, this village was called "Millville" because so many residents worked in its mills.

Eagle Mills, Thomas Wilson, New York, vicinity of Albany, New York, 1845, oil on canvas, 35 ½ x 40 in. Abby Aldrich Rockefeller Folk Art Museum, Colonial Williamsburg Foundation, Williamsburg, Virginia.

MILL GIRLS

{COTTON MILL GIRLS}

There are many variations of this mill-girl song, mostly sung in the American south. But cotton mills were not just a southern phenomena. Spinning and weaving natural fibers is one of the most ancient arts, and cotton mills have existed throughout the industrialized world. The northern mills of Lowell, Massachusetts, were probably the most famous in America. The mill town grew up there, a self-contained industrial community dedicated to maintaining the productivity of the mills. This was also the site of the first mill strike. While the Lowell mill girls worked hard and also educated themselves by going to lectures and reading aloud to one another in the evenings, the cotton mill itself became a kind of symbol for all mills in America.

With a steady lilt (♩ = 82)

I worked in the cot-ton mill all of my life, and I ain't got no-thin' but a Bar-low knife. It's a hard time cot-ton mill girls, It's a

In Peterborough, New Hampshire, during the early 1830s, a young girl named Eliza Gordon was hard at work in the Phoenix Factory, a cotton mill which employed many of the young men and women in her town. When the traveling portrait artists Ruth and Samuel Shute visited Peterborough, the young mill girl dressed in her Sunday best, and sat to have her portrait painted by the popular folk artists.

Eliza Gordon (Mrs. Zophar Willard Brooks), Samuel Addison Shute and Ruth Whittier Shute, Peterborough, New Hampshire, circa 1833, watercolor, gouache, pencil, and ink on paper with applied gold paper, 24 5/8 x 19 in. Collection American Folk Art Museum, New York. Photo by Gavin Ashworth, New York.

Chorus

2. Spinning jennys and cotton gins,
Where one thing ends, the other begins,
It's a hard time, cotton mill girls,
It's a hard time everywhere.
It's a hard time everywhere.
It's a hard time everywhere.
It's a hard time everywhere.
It's a hard time everywhere.

3. When I die, don't bury me at all,
Just hang me up on the spinning room wall,
Pickle my bones in alcohol,
It's a hard time everywhere.
It's a hard time everywhere.
It's a hard time everywhere.
It's a hard time everywhere.
It's a hard time everywhere.

Joseph Yoakum, the creator of this picture, was born on an Indian reservation in Arizona in 1886, but didn't begin to paint regularly until the last decade of his life, the 1960s. During that time he created more than 1,500 watercolors, most of which are landscapes like this picture of a coal mine. Yoakum had no artistic training, and painted what he felt God was telling him to paint. He drew with pens, pastels, pencils, and watercolors on paper. Pastels were his favorite, and he frequently rubbed the pastel colors together to a bright polish that he felt took on the sheen of watercolors.

Sullivan Brothers Coal Mine near Fort Scott Bourbon County, Kansas, Joseph Yoakum, 1966, crayon and pen on paper, 18 1/2 x 24 in. Collection of the National Museum of American Art, Smithsonian Institution, gift of Herbert Waide Hemphill, Jr., and museum purchase made possible by Ralph Cross Johnson, 1986.

MINER

{ DOWN IN A COAL MINE }

The word "collier," meaning miner (and "colliery," meaning the mine and its buildings), came over from England to America, as did many of the miners. This nineteenth-century song, a ballad, has been sung in mining towns for years. Coal has often been referred to as black gold, or dusky diamonds. Mining coal was a dangerous business, for not only were there terrible collapses within the mine that buried miners under heaps of immovable rock, but those who worked too many years underground often came down with fatal lung diseases. Before electricity, the miners used mules or ponies to pull their coal carts. There were mine-tip girls as well, though they are not so well known.

With a carefree spirit (♩=94)

I am a jov-ial col-lier lad, and blithe as blithe can be, For let the times be good or bad, They're all the same to me; 'Tis lit-tle of the world I know and

care less for its ways, For where the dog-star nev-er glows, I wear a - way my days

Chorus

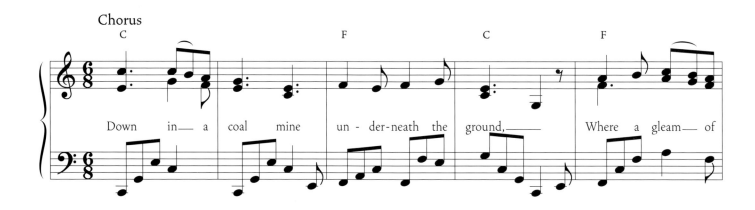

Down in — a coal mine un - der-neath the ground,_____ Where a gleam — of

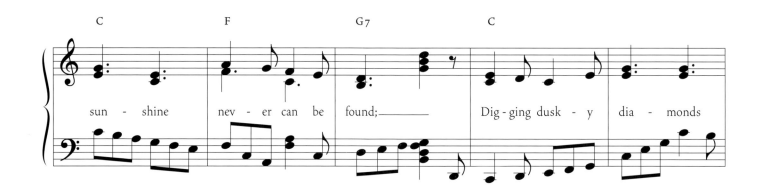

sun - shine nev - er can be found;_____ Dig-ging dusk - y dia - monds

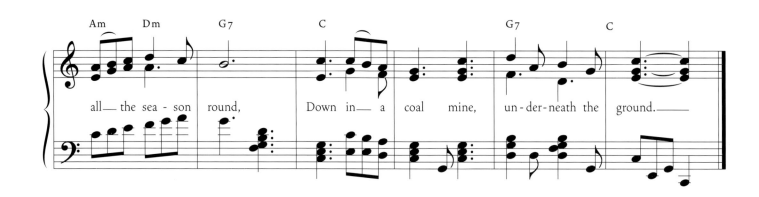

all — the sea - son round, Down in — a coal mine, un-der-neath the ground._____

2. My hands are horny, hard and black,
With working in the vein,
And like the clothes upon my back,
My speech is rough and plain;
Well, if I stumble with my tongue,
I've one excuse to say,
'Tis not the colliers heart that's wrong,
'Tis the head that goes astray.
(Chorus)

3. At every shift, be it soon or late,
I haste my bread to earn,
And anxiously my kindred wait
And watch for my return;
For Death that levels all alike,
Whate'er their rank may be,
Amid the fire and damp may strike,
And fling its darts at me.
(Chorus)

4. But cheer up, lads, and make ye much
Of every joy ye can,
And let your mirth be always such
As best becomes a man;
However Fortune turns about,
We'll still be jovial souls,
What would our country be without
The lads that look for coals.
(Chorus)

During the late 1800s, the discovery of major coal veins in Pennsylvania lead to the opening of many mines and a large demand for workers. This carved wooden figure of a miner was made as a whirligig or wind toy, with movable arms that turned in the wind and a place for a light bulb in his helmet. This strong and muscular miner, with straight posture and eager expression looks like he is ready for a hard day of work in the coal mines.

Figure of a Miner, artist unidentified, Pennsylvania, early 1900s, carved and painted wood with screw socket in the helmet for a light bulb, height 22 ½ in. Photo courtesy of David A. Schorsch—Eileen M. Smiles, Woodbury, Connecticut.

Take up your pen and strike up the band! During the nineteenth century, handwriting was considered an art form, and if you could write with elegant strokes and "flourishes" like these, then you would, no doubt, want to show it off and celebrate with a fanciful drawing like this one.

Demonstration of Penmanship, L. M. Fisher, Lancaster, Ohio, 1880, ink on paper, 22 x 28 in. The Ohio Historical Society, Columbus, Ohio.

MUSICIAN

{THE ORCHESTRA}

This is a traditional song usually sung in classrooms and camps around America. It's fun to make up more stanzas on your own, and to sing it on long car rides. You can vote on who made up the most realistic instrument sounds. What do cymbals sound like?

2. Oh, we can play on the slide trombone,
And this is the music to it:
Too, too, too goes the slide trombone,
And that's the way we do it.

(More verses on the next page.)

3. Fiddle-dee-dee goes the violin,

4. Shake-a-shake-shake goes the tambourine,

5. Pinka-pink-a-pank goes the old banjo,

6. Zum-zum-zum goes the double bass,

7. Blat-a-blat-blat goes the the big brass horn,

8. Tingle-tangle-tink goes the brass triangle.

This figure of a man playing a lute shows the ingenuity often found in American folk sculpture. In about 1900, the Connecticut folk artist Clark Coe used tree limbs, sheet metal, carved wood, and paint to create this unique and amazingly animated sculpture of a musician. Although the artistic style is extremely primitive, we are left with no doubt about the esteem with which the musician holds his beloved instrument.

Musician with Lute, Clark Coe, Killingworth, Middlesex County, Connecticut, circa 1900, paint on pine and ash with metal, 30 x 19 x 22 in. Collection American Folk Art Museum, New York, gift of Museum of Modern Art from the collection of Gordon and Nina Buschaft. Photo by Gavin Ashworth.

PROGRAMMER

{My Father Is a Programmer}

This song was written for this book and is based on Jane's husband (Adam's father), who has spent his working life as a computer scientist. A new song for a new occupation.

Words by Jane Yolen

Music by Adam Stemple

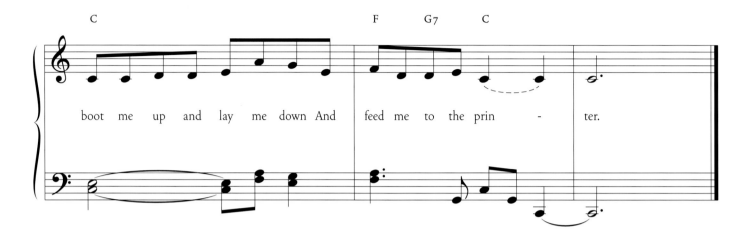

boot me up and lay me down And feed me to the prin - ter.

2. My mother is a programmer,
She programs all day long,
And when she gets up from her screen
She sings this little song:

    Oh, bits and bytes and DOS and RAM,
    They made me all the gal I am,
    So boot me up and lay me down
    And feed me to the printer.

3. But me, I am a hacker
And I hack the whole day long,
And when I get up from my screen,
I sing this little song:

    No bits or bytes can fool my eye,
    No hacker is as smart as I.
    So give it up, I'm on your track,
    You'll never get your data back.

The contemporary artist who made this textile picture was inspired by both folk art and the modern age of computers. Her use of hand stitched letters, numbers, and words comes directly from the English and American folk art traditions of school girl samplers. The combination of this traditional technique with the modern-day subject matter of computers and the Internet results in a dynamic and creative new folk art piece reflecting life in our world today.

Welcome to the Real World, Tilleke Schwarz, the Netherlands, 2001, hand embroidery and stitching on linen, cotton, and silk yarns, 66 x 68 cm. © Tilleke Schwarz, The Netherlands.

RAILROAD ENGINEER

{Casey Jones}

This song was first written about an actual event. It became so popular, it soon gained verses added by various singers, impossible to trace, and new tunes by the dozen. A fireman shoveled coal into the boiler that powered the big steam engines. A switchman was the one who threw the switches so the engine would move to a different track.

With energy (♩ = 105)

Come all you roun-ders, I_____ want you to hear_____ The sto-ry of_____ a_____ brave en-gi-neer;_____ Ca-sey Jones_____ was the

When the railroads started to make their way westward during the 1800s, train stations became the centers of town life and activity. The frenzy and excitement of the arrival of the train is captured in this whimsical cotton appliquéd quilt from Peru, Indiana. The maker chose to use only two colors, and the contrast of blue on white is all that is needed to show the motion of the trains as well as the dynamic energy of the train tracks and railroad station.

Erie Railroad Quilt, artist unidentified, Peru, Indiana, 1888, appliquéd cotton, 78 x 73 in. The Museum of Fine Arts, Boston, Massachusetts.

Chorus

roun - der's name,—— On a big eight wheel - er of a might-y fame.

Ca- sey Jones,—— he pushed on the throt-tle Ca-sey Jones was a brave en-gi-neer,

Come on, Ca-sey and blow the whist-le, Blow the whist - le so they all can hear.

2. Now Casey said, "Before I die,
There's one more train that I want to try,
And I will try ere many a day
The Union Pacific and the Santa Fe."
(Chorus)

3. Caller called Casey about half past four,
He kissed his wife at the station door,
Climbed in his cab and was on his way,
"I've got my chance on the Sante Fe."
(Chorus)

(More verses on the next page.)

This engineer-driven locomotive is unique because most nineteenth-century weathervanes were made in the form of farm animals. It was used on a railroad station in Providence, Rhode Island, in the mid 1800s. It is made of sheet metal, and its charming silhouette evokes the great mobility and progress of its time.

Locomotive Weathervane, unidentified artist, America, circa 1860, sheet zinc, brass rod, iron pipes, and iron bars, 34 in. high. Shelburne Museum, Shelburne, Vermont.

4. Down the slope he went on the fly,
Heard the fireman say, "You've got the white eye."
Well the switchman knew by the engine's moans
That the man at the throttle was Casey Jones.
(Chorus)

5. The rain was a-pounding down like lead,
The railroad track was a river bed,
They slowed her down to a thirty-mile gait,
And the south-bound mail was eight hours late.
(Chorus)

6. Fireman says, "Casey, you're running too fast,
You run the black board last station you passed."
Casey said, "Brother, we're gonna make it through,
For the steam's much better than I ever knew."
(Chorus)

7. Around the curve come a passenger train,
Her headlights shone in his eye through the rain.
Casey blew the whistle with a mighty blast
But the locomotive was a-coming too fast.
(Chorus)

8. The locomotives met in the middle of the hill,
In a head-on tangle that's bound to kill.
He tried to do his duty the yardmen said,
But Casey Jones he was scalded dead.
(Chorus)

Last Chorus:
Casey Jones, he mounted to the cabin,
Casey Jones, his orders in his hand,
Casey Jones, he mounted to the cabin,
Took his final trip to the Promised Land.

The work of twentieth-century folk artist Martin Ramirez is appreciated for its innate sense of design and innovative use of everyday materials. He made this picture by gluing together different types of paper, such as newspaper, candy wrappers, and greeting cards. He created a dynamic tension in this painting by contrasting the still, straight lines of the rails with the curve of the tunnel and the motion of the train. Such sophisticated artistic sensibilities are amazing in a man who was homeless, uneducated, and institutionalized for most of his adult life.

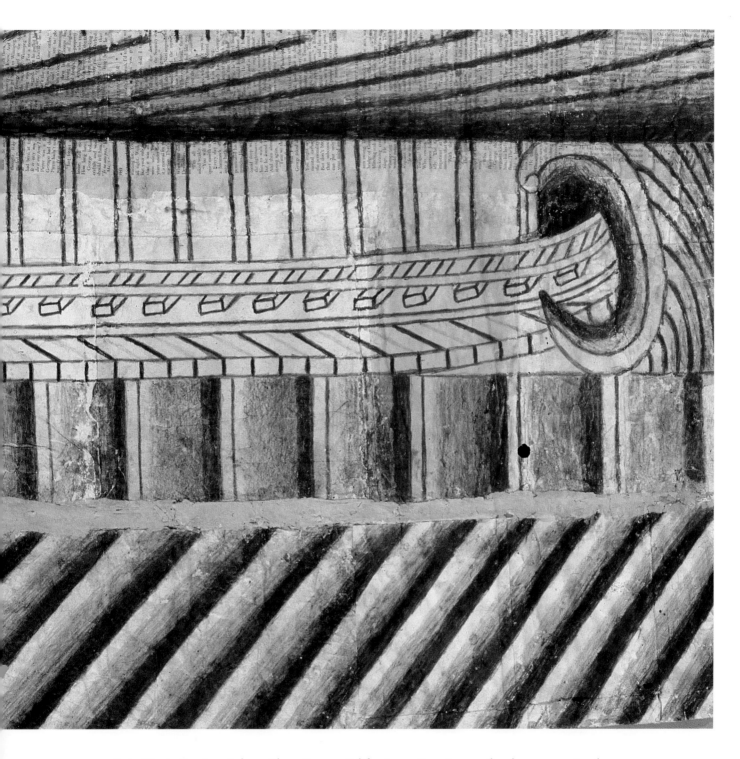

Train, Martin Ramirez, Auburn, Placer County, California, 1948–1960, pencil and crayon on pieced paper, 23 x 46 in. Collection American Folk Art Museum, New York, gift of Herbert Waide Hemphill, Jr. Photo by Gavin Ashworth.

This photograph, taken during the earliest days of photography, gives us a direct view into a typical day of Irish immigrant railway workers. Newly arrived Irishmen worked extremely hard building the American railroad tracks, all for about three dollars per day. These workers are laying the Union Pacific line, part of the first transcontinental railroad. Here they have reached the one hundredth meridian, an imaginary line of longitude that runs north to south, dividing the American east and west.

Laying the Rails of Union Pacific, Kansas, 1866, photograph. Kansas State Historical Society.

RAILWAY WORKER

{Pat Works on the Railway}

When the American railroad system was built in the mid 1800s, many of the men who worked on the tracks were straight off the boat from Ireland. They were called—often derisively—Pat or Paddy. That knickname came from St. Patrick, the patron saint of Ireland, after whom so many Irish people were named. Laying tracks was hard, unrelenting work for little pay, the sort of work immigrants often have to do.

With a plaintive bounce (♩. = 90)

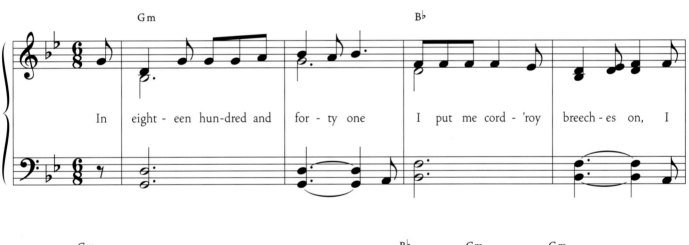

In eight - een hun-dred and for - ty one I put me cord - 'roy breech - es on, I

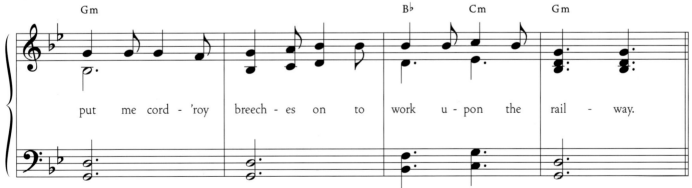

put me cord - 'roy breech - es on to work u - pon the rail - way.

Chorus

2. When we left Ireland to come here,
To spend out latter days in cheer,
Our bosses they did drink strong beer,
While Pat worked on the railway.
(Chorus)

3. The contractor's name was Thomas Ken,
He kept a store to rob the men,
A Yankee clerk with ink and pen
To cheat Pat on the railway.
(Chorus)

4. It's "Pat do this," and "Pat do that."
Without a stocking or cravat,
And nothing but an old straw hat
While Pat works on the railway.
(Chorus)

5. And when Pat lays him down to sleep,
The wiry bugs around him creep,
An' Divil a bit can poor Pat sleep
While he works on the railway.
(Chorus)

6. In eighteen hundred and forty-three,
'Twas then I met sweet Biddy McGee,
An illygant wife she's been to me,
While working on the railway.
(Chorus)

7. In eighteen hundred and forty-six,
They pelted me with stones and bricks,
Oh, I was in a hell of a fix
While working on the railway.
(Chorus)

8. In eighteen hundred and forty-seven,.
Sweet Biddy McGee she went to heaven,
If she left one child, she left eleven
To work upon the railway.
(Chorus)

REAPER

{The Reaper on the Plain}

Written in the middle of the nineteenth century, this song has lyrics by C. G. Eastman, who wrote a number of the most beloved Civil War songs. A reaper cuts and gathers grain for the harvest. On a small farm, the farmer would most likely be the reaper. But on larger farms, many reapers would be hired for the short period of the harvest. Sometimes communities would gather together to help one another bring in the grain, holding harvest feasts afterward. One of the earliest scenes of reaping can be found in the Bible, in the Book of Ruth. Nowadays there are reaping machines that do the work of the many.

Words by C. G. Eastman   *Music by George Frederick Root*

Bend - ing o'er his sick - le 'mid the yel - low grain, Lo! the stur - dy reap - er, reap - ing on the plain; Sing - ing as the sick - le gath - ers to his hand___

This tiny watercolor is only four inches high. It is also very simple in style—everything in the painting is condensed to its bare essence. And yet the painting is both descriptive and lively, a portrait of a typical nineteenth-century rural American farm scene presented with such sensitivity that it was likely painted by one of the farm workers himself.

Farmscape, unknown artist, southeastern Pennsylvania, circa 1810, watercolor on paper, 4 x 3 in. Private collection. Photo courtesy of David A. Schorsch—Eileen M. Smiles American Antiques, Woodbury, Connecticut.

(More verses on the next page.)

2. Long I've stood and ponder'd gazing from the hill,
While the sturdy reaper sung and labor'd still,
Bending o'er his sickle, 'mid the yellow grain,
Happy and contented reaping on the plain.
And as upon my journey I leave the maple tree,
Thinking of the difference between the man and me,
I turn again to see him reaping on the plain,
And almost wish my labor were the sickle and the grain.

Women in rural nineteenth-century America played important roles in the running of both their homes and farms. The vital contributions of women are sometimes seen in the work of American folk artists, who often painted everyday life. This painting depicts a typical midwestern harvest, where grain was being cut and tied by the Illinois region's Scandinavian immigrant settlers.

Harvesting Grain, Olof Krans, Illinois, circa 1900, oil on canvas, 22 ½ x 47 in. Courtesy Bishop Hill Memorial, Illinois Department of Conservation.

RESCUE WORKERS

{BODIES ON THE LINE}

Every era in American history has had disasters and heroes who came to the rescue of those in danger, often as part of their jobs. After September 11, 2001, it became clear that there should be a new song celebrating the heroic work done by the firefighters, paramedics, and others, so here it is.

Words by Jane Yolen

Music by Adam Stemple

During the 1700s and 1800s, the threat of fire was a part of everyday life in American cities. To combat the problem, a system of volunteer fire brigades was created, equipped with engines, ladders, hooks, and leather buckets to fight fires. Those early American firemen were highly respected heroes in their day, just as firefighters are today.

Liberty Company Volunteer Fireman, unidentified artist, Philadelphia, late eighteenth or early nineteenth century, oil on canvas, 24 x 20 in. Private collection.

(*More verses on next page.*)

2. When no one dares, they volunteer,
When no one cares, they still are near.
They do not stop till hope is gone,
And even then they still go on.
Through earthquakes fire, fear, and flood,
They pay the price in sweat and blood.
(Chorus)

Trade figures such as this one were popular in the
nineteenth century. They stood outside shops or on
counters, attracting the interest of customers. This fireman
is small enough to sit on a counter but powerful looking. In
fact, he resembles a celebrated boxing champion of the era,
John L. Sullivan (1858–1918).

Countertop figure of a fireman, Lewis E. Tallier, Roxbury,
Massachusetts, circa 1900, carved and painted white pine,
27 ½ in. high. Private collection. Photo courtesy of David A.
Schorsch—Eileen M. Smiles, Woodbury, Connecticut.

SHOEMAKER

{PEG AN' AWL}

This southern song is a version of an English shoemaker's ditty that dates back to the eighteenth century. In shoemaking, a peg is a pin of wood used to fasten the uppers to the sole or the lifts to each other. An awl is a sharp-pointed tool.

down my pegs, my pegs, my pegs, my awl._____

2. In the days of eighteen and two, (3 times)
Peggin' shoes was all I'd do,
Hand me down my pegs, my pegs, my pegs, my awl.

3. In the days of eighteen and three, (3 times)
Peggin' shoes is all you'd see,
Hand me down my pegs, my pegs, my pegs, my awl.

4. In the days of eighteen and four, (3 times)
I said I'd peg them shoes no more,
Throw away my pegs, my pegs, my pegs, my awl.

5. They've invented a new machine, (3 times)
Prettiest little thing you ever seen,
I'll throw away my pegs, my pegs, my pegs, my awl.

6. Makes a hundred pair to my one, (3 times)
Peggin shoes, it ain't no fun,
Throw away my pegs, my pegs, my pegs, my awl.

This shoe- and bootmaker's trade sign was made during the early 1800s, when many people were still uneducated and unable to read. Made to catch and hold the eye, brightly painted signs such as this one were very effective in showing a largely illiterate public the type of goods or services a merchant was selling.

Josiah Turner Boot Sign, unidentified artist, probably Massachusetts, circa 1810, oil on white pine, 18 3/4 x 44 x 1 2/3 in. Abby Aldrich Rockefeller Folk Art Museum, Colonial Williamsburg Foundation, Williamsburg, Virginia.

Elijah G. Chase

American folk art provides a wealth of documentation of the everyday life of tradespeople during the 1800s. In this watercolor, we are invited into a shoemaker's workshop. The cobbler's friendly eyes draw us into the picture. Folk artists typically lacked technical drawing skills, and yet their work is highly prized for its spontaneous and honest character. In this case, the incorrect perspective is charming, and allows us a glimpse at the top of the cobbler's workbench, where we can see the various tools of his trade drawn in detail.

The Shoemaker, Elijah G. Chase, unidentified artist, Ohio, circa 1840, pencil and watercolor on paper, 11 3/4 x 12 3/4 in. The Columbus Museum of Fine Arts, gift of Edgar William and Bernice Chrysler Garbisch, Columbus, Ohio.

This painted tin sculpture, made in New England in about 1875, was probably used as a trade sign for a traveling vendor. A knife grinder is pictured working at his machine with wheels that actually turned as the little man's legs pushed down. A true piece of buried treasure, this street vendor was found hidden inside the plaster walls of a house in Massachusetts.

Knife Grinder, unidentified artist, probably New England, circa 1875, paint on tin, 13 1/2 x 16 1/4 x 3 1/2 in. Collection American Folk Art Museum, New York, promised gift of Ralph Esmerian. Photo by John Bigelow Taylor, New York.

STREET VENDOR

{Chairs to Mend}

This particular round uses the cries of three separate street vendors. The song has been attributed to Williams Hayes who lived from 1706–1777. In the days when hawkers carried their wares on their backs, they sang out what kind of products they carried. These might be called the earliest commercials.

Words & Music by William Hayes

Chairs to mend, old chairs to mend, Rush or cane bot-tom, old chairs to mend, old

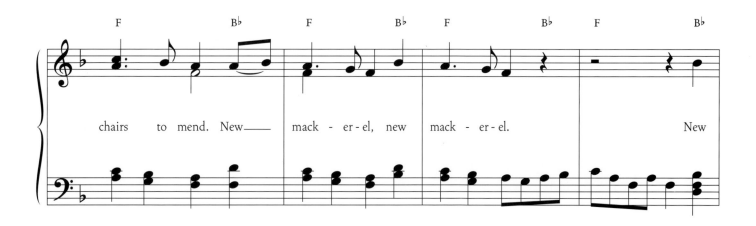

chairs to mend. New mack - er - el, new mack - er - el. New

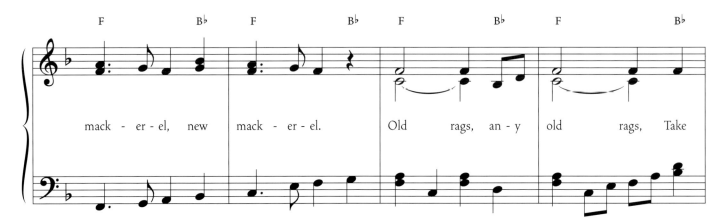

mack - er - el, new mack - er - el. Old rags, an - y old rags, Take

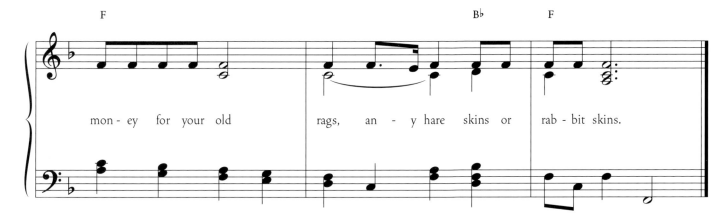

mon - ey for your old | rags, an - y hare skins or | rab - bit skins.

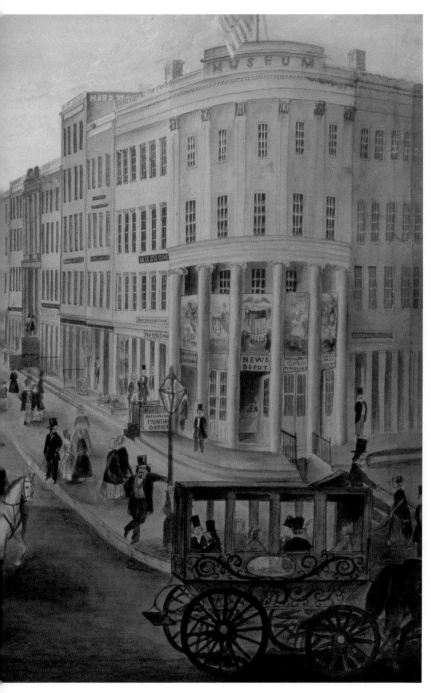

This extraordinarily detailed painting gives us an historical record of daily life during the nineteenth century, as well as a detailed record of downtown Albany, New York, at that time. Shops, banks, printing offices, a museum, a church, and the state capital are all meticulously depicted. Busy shoppers can be seen in the foreground of the painting, examining the goods of a variety of street vendors.

View of State Street, Albany, John Wilson, Albany, New York, 1848, watercolor of paper, 20 ¼ x 28 ¼ in. Albany Institute of History & Art.

The Hoosac Tunnel, built in western Massachusetts in the nineteenth century, took twenty-two years to complete and is almost five miles long. The rock drill, invented in 1865 and wielded by tarriers, helped create this marvel. Tarriers drilled and blasted their way through the Berkshire Mountains, removing twenty million tons of rock.

Hoosac Tunnel for the West, unidentified artist, signed "W.D.", circa 1880/9, full-color print, 56 x 35 cm. Collection of the Library of Congress.

TARRIER

{DRILL, YE TARRIERS, DRILL}

A tarrier is a rockdriller, or a rockdriller's assistant, stationed beside the steam drills to remove loosened rocks. Tarriers worked for the railroads, blasting rocks to lay tracks and create tunnels in hills and mountains for trains to pass through. This song is a popular musical stage number from the late 1800s. It was written by a former tarrier, Thomas Casey, and composer Charles Connolly, and quickly became a favorite among Irish quarry workers.

Words by Thomas Casey

Music by Charles Connolly

With force (♩ = 120)

Ear-ly in the morn-ing at sev-en o'-clock there are twen-ty tar-ri-ers a drill-ing at the rock, And the

Chorus

boss comes a-round and he says, "Keep still, and come down hea-vy on your cast i-ron drill. And

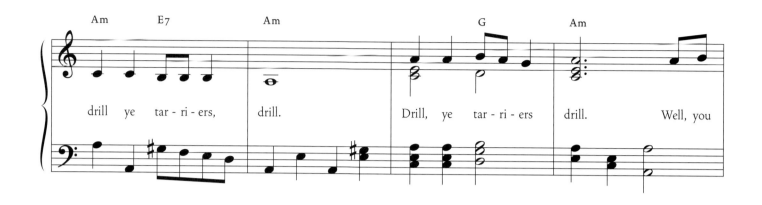

drill ye tar - ri - ers, drill. Drill, ye tar - ri - ers drill. Well, you

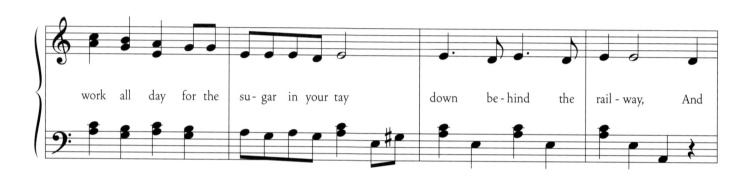

work all day for the su - gar in your tay down be - hind the rail - way, And

drill ye tar - ri - ers, drill, and blast, and fire."

2. Now our new foreman's name was Jim McGann,
By golly, he was a blame mean man.
Last week a premature blast went off,
And a mile in the air went Big Jim Goff.
(Chorus)

3. Now, when next payday came around
Jim Goff a dollar short was found.
When asked what for, came this reply,
"You were docked for the time you were up in the sky."
(Chorus)

TEACHER

{APPLE FOR THE TEACHER}

This is actually a brand-new song written with full knowledge of what teachers go through these days. The lyricist has been a college teacher, the composer is a son and grandson of teachers.

Words by Jane Yolen

Music by Adam Stemple

Regretfully (♩ = 108)

In the good old days when— teach-ers got praised, For ev - 'ry kid who

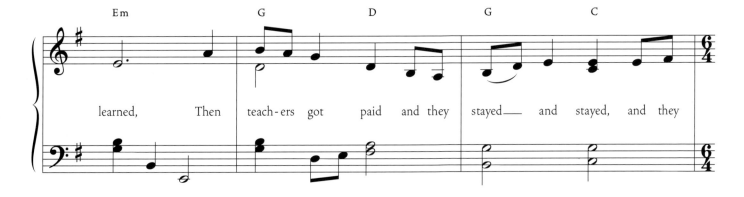

learned, Then teach-ers got paid and they stayed— and stayed, and they

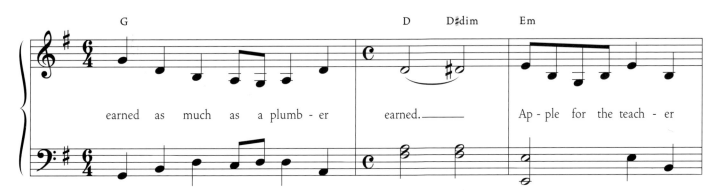

earned as much as a plumb - er earned.— Ap - ple for the teach - er

This watercolor gives us a glimpse inside a typical American one-room schoolhouse, and was probably painted by one of the students. It depicts children of all ages studying on hard, backless benches. The painting tells us about the strictness of the teachers in pioneer schools. The child in the back row is wearing a dunce cap and suffering from a recently boxed ear. The teacher is portrayed as unnaturally large, looming menacingly over the small, crying, and seemingly bored students.

The School Room, Jonathan Jenning, Tioga, Pennsylvania, circa 1840, watercolor, graphite, and colored pencil on paper, 17 x 20 in. Photo courtesy of David A. Schorsch—Eileen M. Smiles American Antiques, Woodbury, Connecticut.

2. In the good old days
When teachers weren't fazed
By big bad boys
And gunlike toys,
Then teachers got paid
And they stayed and stayed
And they earned as much
As a farmer earned.

This carved, wooden sculpture of a worker leading his team of oxen was made in about 1875. The worker seems to have just felled a tree, and is now returning home with a satisfied smile on his face, after a good day's work. The man and oxen are out of scale—the oxen should be much bigger than they are. It is the quirky and somewhat primitive treatment of details, scale, and perspective that add to the charm of this and many other works of American folk art.

Two Pair of Oxen Pulling a Man on a Sledge, midwestern United States, circa 1875, carved wood. From The Henry Ford, Dearborn, Michigan.

TEAMSTERS

{THE OXEN SONG}

The word "teamster" literally refers to ox drivers and their teams of oxen. In the American colonies in the seventeenth century, such teams were used to haul logs out of the deep woods. Since those logging crews were made up of Irish, French-Canadians, and English Yankees, the names in this song reflect that heritage. These days, trucks are used instead of horse or ox teams, and the Teamsters Union is now the world's largest union. It began with the haulers, but today its members span not only truckers and drivers, but laundry workers, brewers, bakers, parking attendants, car rental agents, paper manufacturers, movie and TV workers, and hundreds more.

With purpose (♩ = 85)

Come all you bold ox team-sters___ wher - ev - er you may be, I hope you'll pay at - ten - tion and lis - ten un - to me.

(More verses on next page.)

2. It's of a bold ox teamster,
His name I'll tell to you,
His name was Johnny Carpenter,
He pulled the oxen through.

3. 'Twas early in the season
In the fall of twenty-five;
John Ross he sent four oxen up
For Carpenter to drive.

4. He took with him six bags of meal
And his bunk chains also,
All for to bind his spruce and pine
While hauling through the snow.

5. Says Carpenter unto Flemmons,
"I'll show them how to haul spruce,
For my oxen in the snow, you see,
Are equal to bull moose!"

6. Now the first day we was hauling
We landed forty-nine,

And in a short time after that
We began to fall behind.

7. Sebat he went to Carpenter,
These words to him did say:
"We've got to run another turn,
For this will never pay.

8. "We've got to run another turn,
And we'll all work together;
I've found a wonderful bunch of pine
'Way up at the head of the medder."

9. Now his oxen they have got so poor,
To haul they are not fit.
His sled looks like a butcher block,
All smeared with blood and grit.

10. He tried to keep his oxen fat,
But found it was no use;
For all that's left is skin and bone
And all the horns are loose.

This is one of seventeen banners displayed in parades sponsored by the Maine Charitable Mechanics Association during the early 1800s. Like the teamsters' union, this organization was formed to protect the interests of workers, "mechanics" or skilled craftsmen, such as carpenters, cabinet makers, and smiths. This banner was painted by William Capen of Portland, Maine, and carried by "housewrights" or home builders in the parades.

Parade Banner, William Capen, Maine, circa 1875, painted silk. The Maine Charitable Mechanics Association, Portland, Maine.

TELEPHONE OPERATOR

{LONG DISTANCE BLUES}

This song was written during World War II and was especially popular with the African-American GIs. In those days, making a long-distance phone call always meant getting help from the operator. There were no area codes then, no computer-generated voices, and no touch-tone dials. The operators were almost always women. Today, both men and women work for the phone companies.

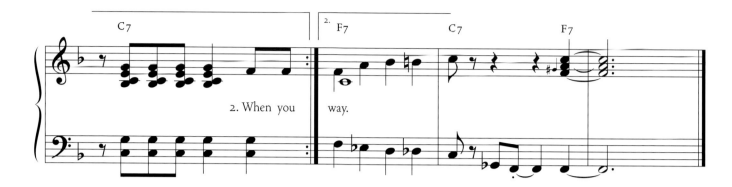

2. When you get her number, tell her what I say,
When you get her number, tell her what I say,
Gonna keep right on ringing to drive my blues away.

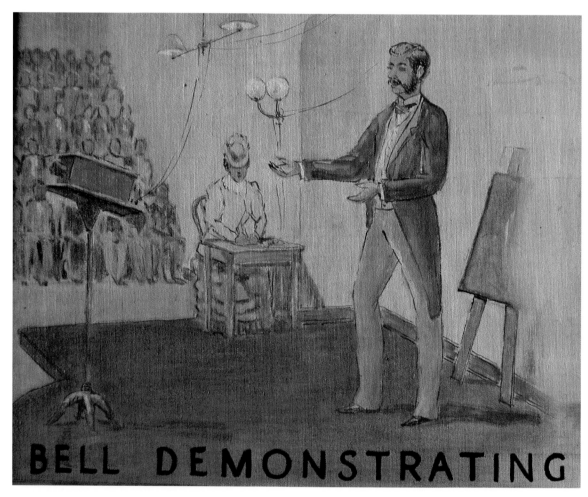

This is part of a group of paintings done in about 1935 as a commemorative series and tribute to early inventors. In this image of Alexander Graham Bell demonstrating his telephone in 1877, we can see the scale and complexity of his enormous first telephone. The woman in the painting is most likely a telephone operator, assisting Bell with his demonstration.

Bell Demonstrating His Telephone, Salem, 1877, unidentified artist, American, circa 1935, oil on canvas, 14 x 34 in. Photo courtesy of Loon Lake, Ltd., Flossmoor, Illinois.

WAIT STAFF

{STAND AND WAIT}

Once people who waited on tables were called waiters and waitresses. Now they are called "wait staff." The job entails hours standing around and carrying heavy trays for low pay. This song was written especially for this book. The line about "they also serve who only stand and wait" is borrowed from a famous poem by John Milton, "On His Blindness," which has nothing to do with wait staffs.

Words by Jane Yolen   *Music by Adam Stemple*

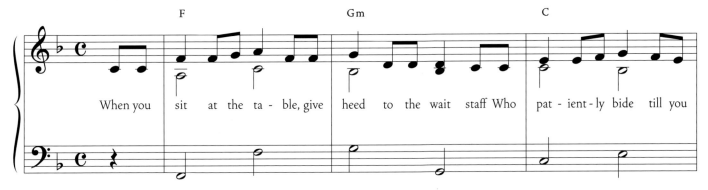

This table rug, or table cover, was made as a useful household decoration. It is so unusual and sculptural, however, that it is now appreciated as a work of art. The three-dimensional qualities of the place settings and plump, juicy fruits are enhanced by the hand-stitched flowers on the platter and plates.

Table Rug, unidentified artist, Pennsylvania, circa 1870, appliquéd cotton and wool. The Schwenkfelder Library, Pennsburg, Pennsylvania.

2. Sometimes it's the kitchen that's slow in preparing,
Sometimes it's the kitchen that overcooks meat.
Don't blame your poor wait staff for all that they bring to you,
Their backs are sore, aching, and so are their feet.
(Chorus)

This sculpture of a seated woman, shown spinning yarn, is a whirligig, or wind toy. These objects were mounted outdoors to reveal the speed and direction of the wind. In this elaborate example, the wind moved both the spinning wheel and the pumping motion of the woman's foot, making her work quickly on a windy day, and frantically during strong gusts.

Spinning Woman Whirligig, unidentified artist, United States, late nineteenth century, carved and painted wood, 28 x 23 ½ x 22 ½ in. Shelburne Museum, Shelburne, Vermont.

WEAVERS

{WEAVE-ROOM BLUES}

The spinners and handloom weavers of the eighteenth century, single men or women working at home, gave way to the great mills with their steam-driven looms. This song about the southern mills, written by Dorothy Dixon, catches the rhythm of those ten-hour days. When a loom went down for repairs, everyone lost wages, so the "fixer"—the one who had to patch things up quickly—looked sore indeed. From *The Lowell Offering*, a journal written by the Massachusetts mill girls comes this complaint about mill work: "Up before day, at the clang of the bell—and out of the mill by the clang of a bell—just as though we were so many living machines."

Words & Music by Dorothy Dixon

Plaintively (♩ = 110)

Work - in' in a weave - room, fight - in' for my life, Tryin' to make a liv - in' for my

kid - dies and my wife, Some are need - in' cloth - in' and some are need - in' shoes—— But

2. With your looms a-slammin', shuttles bouncin' on the floor,
And when you flag your fixer, you can see that he is sore.
I'm tryin' to make a livin' but I'm thinkin' I will lose,
For I'm a-getting' nothin' but them weave-room blues.
(Chorus)

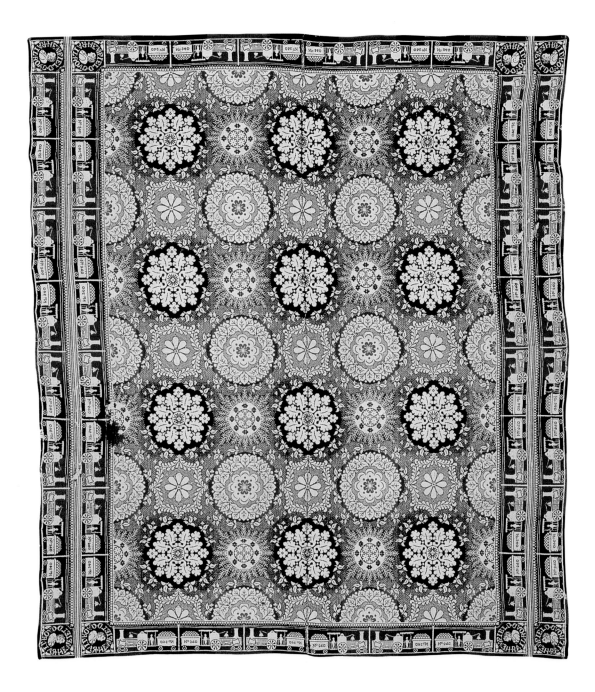

This coverlet was woven on a loom, and its design was predetermined by a series of cards through which holes were punched in the desired pattern. A machine called a jacquard attachment "read" the pattern of punched holes, much like a computer reads our CDs today. Although a machine was involved in the making of this coverlet, an artist with a keen eye designed its lively snowflakes and trains, and a skilled craftsman was needed to work the loom.

Fancy-Weave Doublecloth Coverlet: Snowflake Medallion with Hemfield Railroad Border, unidentified artist, possibly West Virginia or Pennsylvania, 1850–1857, wool and cotton, 90 1/4 x 81 in. Collection American Folk Art Museum, New York, gift of Stephen L. Snow.